M
Sp
Ho

MW01043272

VGM'S
CAREER
PORTRAITS

SPORTS

SPORTS

Julie Rigby

VGM Career Horizons
a division of *NTC Publishing Group*
Lincolnwood, Illinois USA

Photo Credits:

Page 1: Photo courtesy of Stanford University Department of Athletics; pages 15, 29, 43, 57, and 71: Photo Network; page 79: Ray Grabowski/Slapshot Photo.

Library of Congress Cataloging-in-Publication Data

Rigby, Julie.
    Career portraits. Sports/Julie Rigby.
        p. cm.
    ISBN 0-8442-4361-2
    1. Sports—Biography—Juvenile literature. [1. Sports-
-vocational guidance. 2. Vocational guidance. 3. Occupations.]
    I. Title.
    GV697.A1R566   1995
    796'.092—dc20
    [B]   94-15315
                                                CIP
                                                AC

Published by VGM Career Horizons, a division of NTC Publishing Group
4255 West Touhy Avenue
Lincolnwood (Chicago), Illinois 60646-1975, U.S.A.

4 5 6 7 8 9 0 ML 9 8 7 6 5 4 3 2 1

Contents

Take me out to the ball game
Take me out with the crowd
Buy me some peanuts and cracker-jack
I don't care if I never get back!

—Jack Norworth

Introduction

What could be more exciting than being an athlete? Do you think you have what it takes to be a coach? Wouldn't it be great to spend all of your time around sports?

Who says that to grow up you need to give up the things you love most? There are jobs in sports for people with many different kinds of skills. So whether you want to be an athlete, a businessperson, a doctor, a writer, or a teacher, you can find work in the exciting world of sports careers.

ATHLETES

I t's the last game of the season, and your team is down by a point. You get the ball and sink a beautiful jump shot. The crowd goes crazy. Bases are loaded and you step up to bat. You swing, connect, and the fans in the stands go wild. Who hasn't dreamed of living such a moment? Athletes are modern-day heroes, and the great ones are recognized and admired wherever they go. But being an athlete isn't all fun and games. It takes talent, grit, and determination to become a professional athlete.

What it's like to be an athlete

Imagine that you are paid to do something that you would want to do anyway, something that you did for free as a kid. Professional athletes enjoy this privilege. Of course, there are many different levels of athletes, from those who are struggling to make it in the minor leagues to those who are on top of the world, with championship trophies on the shelf and their faces on cereal boxes. Some athletes are individual competitors and shine during the Olympics, while others play and travel with the team. There are as many ways to be an athlete as there are games to play, but there's one thing all athletes have in common: the hours they put into being a top competitor.

The pleasures and pressures of being an athlete

Years after they have stopped playing in a sport, what many athletes remember most fondly is the sense of camaraderie they shared with other athletes. The sense of personal achievement is also important to athletes. But as wonderful as it is to know that you can count on your own skills, even successful athletes face uncertainty and difficulties. A good player can get traded as managers try to create a well-rounded team. Constant travel can be hard on you and your family. The threat of injury always hovers over an athlete's career. And fame can be a double-edged sword. Sometimes privacy is hard to come by if you are very famous.

Preparing yourself to be an athlete

There's really only one way to prepare to become an athlete, and that's to train your body and your mind. The best athletes have active, healthy childhoods, and frequently participate in more than one sport when they are young. It's important, however, that your training not cause more harm than good. Weight lifting is not advised before you reach puberty, and even then it is best to work with light weights and go for repetition. Take extra care to warm up before exercising, and make sure you wear any protective gear associated with your sport. It isn't worth hurting yourself before you even get a shot at fulfilling your dreams.

Becoming a professional athlete

Becoming an athlete is not like preparing for other careers. The best path, though, is the one that prepares you for your life beyond athletics—attending college through graduation. Players who have a college degree have a better chance of going further in their sport and in other areas of work, once their playing days are over.

Many colleges and universities offer scholarships to promising young athletes and scholars. Every year the professional sports organizations hold drafts, and the different teams get a chance to sign up the players they want. In other sports, such as gymnastics and swimming, athletes try out for a place on the U.S. Olympic Team.

Is being an athlete right for you?

To succeed, you need to understand your own reasons for wanting to be an athlete. Most people begin playing sports without really thinking about it. It's what everybody does, it's fun, and exercise is good for you. But there's a big difference between wanting to be on the team because you want to be popular and wanting to achieve a personal goal. There's nothing wrong with wanting to gain prestige and respect through your athletic abilities. Just remember that becoming a professional athlete requires tremendous commitment and sacrifice.

Things you can do now

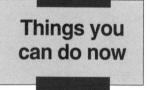

- Study the sport you want to play. The more informed you are, the better able you are to come up with the right response at the right time.

- Keep a sports diary. Every evening, write down everything

you did to improve your performance, such as how long you practiced or how far you ran. If you work with a coach, write down any comments you receive from him or her.

- Get your parents involved. They might not be able to attend every game, but the more you are able to share your interests and ambitions with them, the more they will be able to help and encourage you.

Let's Meet...

Cal Eldred
Baseball Player

Cal Eldred started playing baseball when he was 4 years old. When he was 21 he was drafted as a pitcher in the first round by the Milwaukee Brewers.

Do you think of baseball as a job?

When you are out on the field it's not a job. It's fun and intense, and it's a game. But it's a serious game. Day to day, when I'm off the field, it feels like more of a job. The hardest days are the days that I'm not pitching but doing the training. On those days I'll go to the ballpark and work out for 4 or 5 hours.

What do you like most about being a ballplayer?

This is what I want to do, and I know that not all people get to do what they want to do. I also like the team mentality. If your first interest is the team, then 99 percent of the time you are going to do what's best for the team. And what's best for the team will also be what's best for you. Traveling with the team you learn to enjoy your teammates, and you learn a lot about people.

What do you like the least?

I travel too much, and it's hard not being with my family. During the season I live in Milwaukee, but half of the time I'm on the road. During spring training I'm away from home for 2 months. The only time that you can live where you want to is during November, December, and January.

What do you think it takes to succeed in baseball?

The people who are successful have confidence. There's a lot of pressure in the game, but it comes from what you put on yourself. You can avoid that by having confidence, which comes from being able to sit back and think as well as from physical training. Good ballplayers are also hard workers who are willing to make sacrifices.

Do you ever think about what you will do after baseball?

I think about it every day. When I stop playing I want to spend a lot of time with my family, and with my wife, who's going to be a schoolteacher. I'd like to live more of a normal life, and I would probably finish college, because I left after my junior year.

Do you have any advice for students who want to be athletes?

I'd tell them to use their brains, but I'd also say that they should do what they want to do. No one should ever tell kids that they can't be what they want to be. If they have a dream it can happen.

A Rookie's Year

In 1992, Cal Eldred was something of a "super-rookie" and earned *The Sporting News* Rookie Pitcher of the Year award. Here are some highlights from his first year:

- Was a key member of the starting rotation (14 games; won 11, lost 2, 1.79 earned run average).

- Won 10 games in his first 12 starts.

- Set a club record with an .846 winning percentage.

- Had a ten-game winning streak from August 8 through September 29. Cal tied a club record with Chris Bosio. It was the best streak in the major leagues that year.

- Led his team in winning percentage and earned run average.

- Pitched two complete games and won them both.

- Pitched six or more innings in 13 of 14 starts (93 percent) and seven or more in 11 of 14 starts (79 percent).

- Struck out 12 batters in a 3–1 win over Baltimore, the most strikeouts in a game by a Brewers pitcher in 1992.

- Was named American League Pitcher of the Month for September 1992.

Let's Meet...

Lindsey Hunter
Basketball Player

Lindsey Hunter is a basketball player with the Detroit Pistons. He played basketball at Jackson State University, and graduated with a degree in elementary education in 1993.

When did you start playing basketball?

I've been playing sports all my life. My father and my uncle played basketball; everybody in the family participated in some kind of sport. My first love was football, and I really didn't get serious about basketball until junior high school. Eventually that's the sport that I chose, and I fell in love with it.

What was your routine as a college basketball player?

We practiced every day. We would usually get done with classes at 12:50 and then practice from 1:00 until 4:30. I also worked out every day with weights and sprint training. It was very stressful because in order to play you had to excel at your books. One had to go with the other. You had to perform at both levels and distribute your energies.

What do you like the most about being a basketball player?

Just the fact that I'm out there makes me feel good. I smile a lot when I'm playing. I love it when the crowd gets into the game, and it makes me feel very special. It's a feeling that you can't explain, but it's the reason I play.

What does it take to succeed as a basketball player?

You have to be strong mentally, because things won't always go your way. You need to be strong enough to say "I'm just going to keep working until I find some success at this." The top players, like Michael Jordan, Tim Hardaway, Isiah Thomas, and Joe Dumars, all have a certain air about themselves. It's a good air, like they are down to earth and very human. Everybody puts them on a pedestal like they are gods or something, but they know where they came from and that the fans are the reason they are where they are today.

What does it take to succeed off the court?

You need to keep a level head and realize that you'll always be a human being. That's something that a lot of people don't think about. You might be a superstar, but you're still a human and you were one before you became a professional basketball player. You're just one injury away from being normal again.

Do you have any advice for young athletes?

I always tell kids that they should get a degree first and accomplish something positive that way. You always will need a degree.

From College to the Pros

Lindsey describes the process of being drafted to play professional basketball.

"When the college season ended, it was a slap in the face. It was like, 'You are no longer a college player, it's time to be a professional.' It was hard for me to understand. I was treating things like I was still in college. But everything was different, and everybody was approaching me differently.

"My first step was to get an agent. I had made the decision already to go with Hank Thomas, because I was comfortable talking to him. I felt he was really down to earth and understood what I stood for. Then the draft came along. There are two rounds. I was lucky enough to be drafted in the first round—in the top ten picks—which is pretty good for a 6-foot-2-inch guard.

"On draft day we were at the draft in Detroit, and I was picked by the Pistons. We were sitting out in the room, and they called my name. Right then, I didn't know what I was feeling. I was happy, and I also felt like I wanted to cry. All types of thoughts went through my mind right then. I couldn't believe I was finally there after all those years of dreaming about it."

Success Stories

Shannon Miller   Shannon Miller started gymnastics when she was 5 years old, when her parents brought home a trampoline for Christmas. By the time she was 8, Shannon was training with a gymnastics coach, and quickly became one of the top gymnasts in the country. At the 1992 Summer Olympics in Barcelona, Spain, Shannon won two silver medals and three bronze medals. She was 15 years old, and the shortest (4 feet, 6 inches) and lightest (69 pounds) athlete on the U.S. team. Although Shannon is quiet when off the gym floor, her attitude on the floor is bold and confident.

Frank Thomas   Frank Thomas, first baseman for the Chicago White Sox, is one of the most powerful hitters in baseball today, and also one of the highest paid. At 6 feet 4 inches, and 257 pounds, he is also one of the game's biggest. What makes Frank a superstar is his fantastic hand-eye coordination, and pitchers who face him know he rarely takes a swing at a bad pitch. Despite his popularity and success as a player since he joined the White Sox in 1990, Frank has held onto his easygoing manner. During his fantastic 1993 season, Frank put a piece of tape in his locker that said "DBTH," for "Don't believe the hype."

 When Wayne Gretzky was 6 years old, it took him all year to score a single goal for his hockey team in Brantford, Ontario. When he was growing up, his mother even substituted a bed sheet for living room curtains to pay for his skates. Now the highest-paid player in hockey, the center for the Los Angeles Kings has broken more than 60 records, including most National Hockey League goals in a season (92). He has scored the most career NHL goals and is the all-time NHL assist leader.

Find Out More

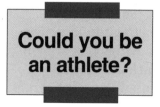

Could you be an athlete?

There's no one way to determine if you are destined to be an athlete. Physical ability is obviously important, but so is a winning attitude. How do you measure up? Is there anything you should work on?

1. Self-confidence. Are you confident in your own ability to learn new skills and perform successfully?

2. Ambition. Do you have the desire to excel, improve, and succeed?

3. Discipline. Are you willing to work hard now for future rewards? Can you make a commitment to developing your potential?

4. Mental toughness. Can you withstand criticism, setbacks, and stress?

5. Self-sufficiency. Are you able to motivate yourself? Do you trust the decisions you make?

6. Leadership skills. Can you take charge in difficult situations? Do the people around you trust you?

7. Open-mindedness. Are you accepting of new people and ideas? Are you willing to listen and learn from your mistakes?

COACHING

Y ou've seen coaches pacing up and down on the sidelines, conferring with players during time-outs and talking on television after their wins and losses. You probably have already come to recognize different coaching styles—like the quiet, laid-back style of Cito Gaston of the Toronto Blue Jays to the aggressive manner of Mike Ditka, a former coach of the Chicago Bears. But how much do you know about what coaches do when they are not in the public eye?

The duties of a coach

Coaches are involved in many aspects of managing a team. On large university and professional teams, the coach will have assistants to handle various aspects of the job. But for smaller teams the coach has a wider range of duties. For example, the basketball coach at a small college is responsible for finding and developing the players for the team. He or she must go out and recruit players, evaluate their skills, coach them on the court, and oversee their academic progress. The coach of a college team must also take care of schedules and travel arrangements. He or she will also be called upon to help with fund raising for the school, attend conference meetings, and make sure that the school is meeting National Collegiate Athletic Association regulations.

The pleasures and pressures of the job

One of the greatest pleasures of being a coach is watching your team compete and win. If you are a fine coach, you will be able to create a team that rises above the raw talents of the individual players. Coaches share the glory when the team wins, and some professional coaches become celebrities themselves. But if the team is losing, more often than not it is the coach who gets blamed. Being a coach is a profession that takes a lot of energy and sacrifice. The hours are long and demanding, and coaches frequently work evenings and weekends. Coaches travel a great deal, both with the team and when recruiting. The starting salary of an assistant coach is low. You need to put in a lot of extra effort to work your way up in this very competitive field.

Climbing the coaching ladder

One of the best ways to prepare to be a coach is to play the game yourself. Many famous coaches played their sport through college and professionally. A typical career for a football coach might begin with coaching at a college. To become a college coach, it is important that you have a college degree; many schools require coaches to have graduate degrees as well. When they make the switch to coaching a professional team, they usually start off as an assistant coach, with a specialization such as defensive end coaching. To make it into the narrow ranks of head coach, you must be good at public relations and show strong leadership and organizational skills.

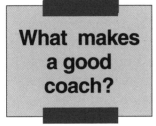

What makes a good coach?

The best way to understand what makes a good coach is to paint a portrait of a bad coach. One of the greatest failures of poor coaches is that they are unable to teach their athletes. They might fail as teachers because they cannot communicate their ideas well, or because they seem to lack the knowledge of what should be done. Impatient people often make bad coaches, and a coach who is unwilling to accept responsibility will try to cover over his or her mistakes by blaming the athletes. So what makes a good coach? A good coach will be a person who takes the long view, who is disciplined and fair, and who is confident in his or her ability to make decisions.

Now decide if coaching is right for you

Do you think you have what it takes to be a good coach? There are certain abilities you must acquire if this is the path you want to follow:

- Expertise in the rules, strategies, and teaching methods of the sport you want to coach

- Knowledge of the safety guidelines for your sport

- An understanding of the best ways to train and condition athletes in your chosen sport

- Familiarity with first aid

- The ability to understand and motivate other people

Let's Meet...

Mark Anthony Person
High School Basketball Coach

Mark Person is the head of the varsity basketball program at Provincetown High School in Massachusetts. He coaches the players from grades nine through twelve.

How did you get your current job?

I moved to Provincetown about 7 years ago, and was hired to coach the junior varsity team. I wanted to start at the bottom and work my way up, so I coached that team for 4 years. Although I'd played basketball and competed, I wanted to learn the philosophy of the game. Later they needed a varsity coach and I moved right up.

Why did you want to coach?

I played basketball in high school and got a scholarship to college, but I realized that I didn't want to go on to try to make it professionally. I felt the chances were very slim to get a spot on a team. I realized that I had talent as a coach when I was coaching an intramural team in college, and so I put my energies into that.

How did you learn to be a coach?

I learned a lot from the coaches that I had in high school and college. I've played with a number of great players, including some who are in professional ball now. I coach more from these great learning experiences than from what I've read in a book.

What does it take to be a good high school basketball coach?

You have to treat all student athletes fairly. You need to be honest with them, when times are good or bad. You also must be committed to the job, and be prepared when you come to practice. If you are, the kids will back you all the way when the game is on the line. You have to be the kind of person they can depend on and trust. I'm a very disciplined coach, and I want to pass that on to the students. From a purely coaching standpoint, you need to know your opponents and how you can actually beat them.

What do you like most about your job?

The most important part of the job doesn't have to do specifically with basketball, but with teaching the students about life in general. I think the experiences they'll have playing basketball will stay with them for the rest of their lives, and make them compete in business and a lot of other aspects in life. I get a lot of enjoyment from seeing the players execute what I've been teaching them. But I don't think winning is that important. What's more important is that the kids learn more about life.

Building a Winning Team

The school on Cape Cod where Mark Person coaches is the smallest one east of the Mississippi River. It's no wonder that every team they play is supposed to beat them. So how does Mark motivate his players?

"When I started here, I came to a program that hadn't won a game in 5 years. People told me I should be prepared to lose. But I'm a positive thinker and I wanted to bring this program some respectability. So I did what I needed to do—my way—and it worked out. We beat a team that we hadn't beaten in 10 years, and that gave me a lot of enjoyment. It was a turning point for me to know that I could be successful, that we could compete against larger and better teams. The pinnacle was that the kids I coached as freshmen went on as seniors to the semifinals of the state championships.

"I try to teach them from my own life experiences. I'm the only black coach in our conference, the Cape and Islands League, and I'm also the youngest coach. So there have been times I've felt alienated. I like to face up to challenges, and I try to pass that on to the kids. The Cape is a very small place, I tell them, and you are going to need to compete for jobs when you go into the city. This is good preparation for life."

Let's Meet...

Mary Toole
Tennis Instructor

Mary Toole has been a tennis instructor since 1981. She is a licensed physical therapist with a master's degree in special education. She has been the director of a program for developmentally disabled children for 19 years.

How did you get started in tennis?

When I was around 14 my mom brought home a racket from her domestic job. I went out to the neighborhood courts and sat there until I got the courage to ask someone to hit with me. I fell quickly in love with tennis. It gave me a structure. I went to study in the physical therapy program at Northwestern, and after graduation I started playing tennis daily. I joined the oldest black tennis club in the United States, and met a lot of seasoned tennis players. I competed for 12 years, and I was even rated as an "A" player.

How did you start teaching?

My daughter got involved in a junior tennis program. I found myself getting annoyed at what seemed like a disorganized program. One day someone said to me, "Why don't you get down and do something about it?" So I did. At first I was teaching on a volunteer

basis. Later I went on to develop a Tiny Tot
Tennis program for a local tennis club, to get
kids started at a very early age.

Do you have a particular method of teaching?

I teach the 3 C's: control, confidence, and
coordination. I'm always saying to kids, "If we
control our bodies we control the ball." I help
my students build up their confidence. I tell
them that if you put forth your best you can do
it. I can also use my background as a physical
therapist to improve any child's coordination.
With very young children I do a lot of activities
without the racket to get them warmed up,
and to work on their coordination. We have
rolling races, snake-tight movements, 360s in
the air, walking and running backwards. It's a
rare kid who doesn't fall down, but they are
usually laughing. Then we move on to the
racket work.

Do you have a teaching philosophy?

I feel I'm teaching the game of tennis and not
just how to hit a ball. I'm known for setting
goals and making demands of the kids. Not
everybody likes that. But that's my style. I
have expectations and I will encourage kids to
have expectations themselves. I ask kids: Do
you have any goals? If you are just out here to
have fun, fine, I can have fun. But no one
accomplishes anything if you don't invest in it.
Most kids can make a commitment to doing
well and improving, but it has to come from
the kid, not from the parents or the teacher.

What kind of pressure do you feel?

Sometimes the competition between the kids is hard to handle. They can tell who is hitting better, who is learning faster. So I try to be conscious of what each child is trying to do, and I'll compliment each one for his or her ability. Kids are competitive, and this is a competitive sport. Sometimes that's hard on children.

What do you like about teaching tennis?

What's most satisfying for me is to see the students grow as individuals and get in touch with themselves. Sports give you a center, whether you are a kid or an adult. Sports also give you a sense of mastery and creativity. And I like being part of that.

The Personal Side of Being a Tennis Coach

For Mary Toole, being a coach can be a very personal experience. For the children she coaches, the lessons learned on the court sometimes have as much to do with being a person as with being a tennis player. Here is an experience Mary had as a coach that reminded her of how her involvement with students goes beyond simply teaching tennis.

"Once I had to tell a father to go home. He was complaining about his own son's game, and was putting too much pressure on the kid. The kid kept looking out at the side of the court, looking really sad. It was throwing him off, taking away his confidence. I went over to the father and told him that he had to go home. And after the game I went over to their house and embraced the father. 'Thank you for letting your son win,' I told him.

"The experience of kids playing tennis is a family commitment. I'm glad to be part of their lives. I think my voice gets inside them. They can hear my voice while they're playing. And I can work on making sure that the parents give them the same message: a message of encouragement."

Danny Mack Gable

When Dan Gable was in high school and college he was the country's finest amateur wrestler, winning 181 matches before his first loss in the NCAA finals in 1970. From there he went on to win the gold medal in the 1972 Summer Olympics in Munich without giving a single point to his opponents. He went to work as a wrestling coach at the University of Iowa in 1977, and was named the NCAA Rookie Coach of the Year. Since then he has led his Hawkeyes to repeated NCAA championships. When he coached the U.S. Olympic team in 1984, American wrestlers won seven gold and two silver medals. He is in the U.S. Wrestling Hall of Fame and the U.S. Olympic Hall of Fame.

L. Margaret Wade

Coach Wade started as a player in her high school in Mississippi and played basketball in college at Delta State University. After graduation she was a high school coach before going back to Delta State in 1973 to build a championship team. Margaret Wade was not only a phenomenal coach who was able to attain a career record of 633 wins and only 117 losses before retiring in 1979, she was also a pioneer for women's basketball. In 1975, she became one of only three women inducted into the Basketball Hall of Fame in Springfield, Massachusetts.

Find Out More

You and coaching

A good coach is an informed coach. There are things you can do now to prepare yourself for a future in coaching.

- Study your sport. This may sound obvious, but only a complete knowledge of your sport will allow you to choose the best strategies. Pay special attention to any rule changes or other developments that could affect your strategy.

- Learn as much as you can about physical conditioning for your sport.

- Learn about the jobs of various people associated with your sport: scorekeepers, officials, managers.

- Volunteer to serve as a referee or umpire at lower-level competitions (like Little League).

- Even better, volunteer to work as a coach for younger children at your school or neighborhood center.

- Ask the coaches at your school or neighborhood club if you can attend their practices. Compare the various styles and methods of coaching. During a game, pay special attention to the kinds of decisions coaches need to make. When do they substitute players? How do they get their athletes to focus?

- Look for books and magazine and newspaper articles on coaching your sport. Articles may be found in general interest sports magazines, in magazines that cover only one sport, and in coaching magazines. Keep a file of articles that you think will be useful to you later.

- Are there any professional coaches you admire? Write to their organizations for public relations material or any coaching guidelines they have written.

SPORTS

COMMUNICATIONS

H ow would you like to have a great seat at a championship basketball game, hang out in the locker room after the Super Bowl, or go to the ballpark every day? That's what people who have jobs in sports communications get to do. They are the writers, sportscasters, radio announcers, photographers, camera operators, and public relations specialists who give us the latest scores and action and who tell us about our favorite players. It may be a dream job, but bringing sports news to the public is still a job.

Jobs in sports communications

Large newspapers and magazines hire reporters to cover the sports beat. At a smaller newspaper, reporters are often on general assignment and may report on other local events in addition to sports.

Sportscasters are hired by radio and television stations. They may work for a local newscast or a national sports show, doing play-by-play coverage or sports commentary and analysis.

Photographers capture the vivid moments of a game for newspaper and magazine readers. Camera operators work for television and cable stations.

Public relations specialists are hired by sports teams. Their job includes handling questions from the media about the team and the players, arranging press conferences, and writing news releases.

What it's like to work in this field

Many reporters, sportscasters, photographers, and camera operators lead very irregular lives. They might go to work in the middle of the day, and not be home until the middle of the night. They often travel with the team they are covering, bringing the sports news to their hometown. They work with the editors at the newspaper or the producers at the television station, communicating by phone, fax, and computer. Public relations specialists generally work more regular hours, but this can vary according to the team or the sport.

The pleasures and pressures of the job

A reporter or photographer might have the best seat in the stadium or the ballpark, but you can bet they aren't eating hot dogs and doing the wave. For many people in the media, one of the greatest pleasures of their jobs is that they get to interact with the athletes and coaches off the field. They also enjoy the company of their fellow reporters. The most difficult part of working in the media is the strict deadlines. There is tremendous pressure to get the story out right away. After all, your story isn't too interesting if it appears the day after every other paper has printed it.

Is working in sports communications right for you?

If you are a person who can't imagine being locked in an office all day, this might be the right line of work for you! To be good in this field you need to have a love of sports and be willing to put in crazy hours. You also need to be observant and accurate. You need to meet deadlines, take responsibility for your own work, and be willing to accept criticism from editors and other people you work with.

Which job is right for you?

There are many different ways of communicating. Which way suits you best?

- Do you enjoy speaking in public, telling stories, and finding new ways to describe things? If so, you might make a good sports-caster.

- Do you like to write down what you hear and observe? Do you enjoy gathering information and writing reports? You might have a future as a reporter.

- If you are a more visual person and enjoy art and photography, you might be happy behind a camera.

- Are you an outgoing person? To be a public relations specialist you must be organized, enthusiastic, and have very good communication skills.

The importance of experience

Melissa Isaacson, a sportswriter we'll meet in this chapter, offers this advice for budding reporters. "It's never too early to start. Try to get as much experience as possible. In high school you can get a job at the local newspaper emptying wastepaper baskets. You'll have a leg up on

everybody else your age. And who
knows what you might pick up?
After a couple months they might
let you answer the phones. Then
they might let you write a little. As
soon as you know what you want to
do, try to do it. Get your feet wet
and find out if you really like it.
Start gaining experience, which is
how you get jobs."

Let's Meet...

Melissa Isaacson
Sportswriter

Melissa Isaacson writes about the Bulls for the *Chicago Tribune*. It's her responsibility to cover everything that happens to the basketball team and to the individual players.

How did you become a sportswriter?

I started by taking introductory journalism classes and working for small newspapers. I was the assistant editor of the college newspaper at the University of Iowa, where I also covered basketball. I got my first job for a medium-size paper in Florida, and covered high school sports and the Tampa Bay Buccaneers. From there I went to *USA Today*, where I was a general assignment reporter, and then to the *Orlando Sentinel* for four years, where I was a columnist and covered Florida State football and basketball, among other things. I came to the *Chicago Tribune* in 1990, and in 1991 got the Bulls beat.

What is a typical game day like?

I get to the stadium at 5 P.M. for a 7:30 game. At around 6 P.M., the locker room opens for 45 minutes and the reporters are allowed in

there to talk to the players. It's a weird work-
day. I don't leave the house until 4 P.M. and
usually don't get home until after midnight.

When do you write your story?

I work on a computer in the press box, and I
write most of the story during the second half.
My first deadline is 10:30. Usually that's after
the game is over, but if the game runs long,
I've got to write the story so that it could go
either way and they can just plug the score in
at the office. After the game, I need to run
down to the locker room and talk to the
coaches and players. Then I run back up and
rewrite the story using quotes.

How does it get to the morning paper?

My computer is connected to the office computer, and I transmit the story by phone line.
The editors have only about 10 minutes to
check it over and write the headline.

What do you like the most about your job?

I enjoy the variety. There are no two days that
are the same. Also, you know for a fact that a
lot of people are really counting on you to tell
them what's going on. It's a little scary, but it's
really exciting.

Do you travel a lot?

I go to every game, with few exceptions. The
Bulls average about 100 games a season,
which adds up to about 45 games on the road.
Sometimes the traveling can be too much.
Last year was the first year in 10 years that I
was home for Thanksgiving.

Covering a Championship Team

When Melissa Isaacson was interviewed for this book the Bulls had recently won their third world championship. What is it like to cover such a popular team?

"I've been a sportswriter for 11 years, and when this is your job you can get a little jaded. But I realize that years from now Michael Jordan will still probably be considered the greatest basketball player ever. As a sportswriter I feel really blessed to have watched such a great team.

"People think that if you are on the beat you are a fan, and that you are rooting for the Bulls. I'm a fan, but as a reporter I am rooting for the story. You do spend a lot of time with the players and you do start to root for them. You know how hard they have worked. It's a great story for them to win, but sometimes losing stories are just as good.

"The first championship I covered was the Bulls' second one. I remember just standing on the court of the stadium that night and watching the players coming back onto the court and dancing on the table. I was on deadline, but for a second I just stood there and took it all in—not as a reporter, but just as a person. It was an incredible experience, like climbing into your TV set. At times like that you think, this is really a fun job."

Let's Meet...

John Kringas
Sports Photographer

John Kringas is a staff photographer for a large newspaper. Before he got that job, he sold pictures to magazines, newspapers, and news services.

What does it take to be a photographer?

You need to be accurate, truthful, and ethical. You also need to be very resourceful. Every picture has a story behind it, and a good photographer can tell that story. One of the most important things you need to do is understand the story you are covering, so you can translate that into a visual image. For example, let's say Patrick Ewing makes the greatest shot ever at the end of a game. You need a picture of that.

What is a typical day for you?

I work out of my car, which is like my office. An hour or so before my shift starts I call up the assignment desk at the newspaper, in case there is something that they need me to do immediately.

By 9 A.M. all the photographers are in their cars. We have two-way radios in our cars, like police radios.

Is it hard to get your job?

There is a lot of competition and not a lot of jobs. For example, a few universities graduate 150 to 200 students in photojournalism a year. Maybe 25 or 30 of them are fortunate to find a job as a newspaper photographer, and only a few of them at a big city paper.

What is it like taking pictures at a basketball game?

If there is an important game, with a 7:30 P.M. tip-off, you need to get to the stadium by 5 P.M. The NBA assigns spots to the photographers, so you'll know your position. Then you do what you need to do to get ready, like setting up your equipment. You look for anything out of the ordinary once you are there.

What do you like about your job?

I like the people I'm around. I'm fascinated by history, and in this job I get to see and record history. I know that one day these pictures will have historical significance. No other medium is as frozen in time as a newspaper. For me, photography is also my best tool for communication.

Is there anything you don't like?

Sometimes I don't get the picture I want. I think photographers are the greatest complainers in the world; nothing is ever right. I don't even hang my pictures in my house, because I'm never fully satisfied with my work. It also bothers me when I shoot a picture that I really like, and then it doesn't make the paper.

Sports Photography: Science and Art

As John Kringas puts it, to be a sports photographer, "You don't just go out and snap away." If you think that to get a good picture you need only to be in the right place at the right time, you're wrong. While luck might get you a few amazing pictures, it takes preparation and planning to be a successful sports photographer. To succeed you must be able to capture the actions and emotions of sports competitions day after day.

A winning sports photographer will have:

- A knowledge of photographic techniques
- The ability to choose the right equipment and film for the job
- A familiarity with the sport being photographed
- A "sixth sense" to anticipate what might happen next.

What makes an exciting photograph varies from sport to sport. Sometimes it's the slide into a stolen base, or the look of intense concentration on a pitcher's face. At a track race some of the best pictures come at the turn or at the finish line. If you know that a particular tennis player likes to rush the net, you might be able to capture a stunning overhead smash. The more you know about the sport you are photographing, the better you'll be at guessing what might happen next.

Success Story

George Brace

When George Brace was 10 years old, he discovered something he liked as much as playing baseball: photography. George, born in 1913, was a baseball fanatic, and it wasn't long before he was bringing his camera with him on the 20-mile walk from the South Side of Chicago to watch the Chicago Cubs play ball at Wrigley Field. By the time he was a teenager, George was hanging out in the locker room, talking to such baseball greats as Lou Gehrig and Babe Ruth and asking if he could take their picture. George got his lucky break in 1929, when he got to know George C. Burke, the official photographer for the Chicago Cubs. Burke asked George if he would like to work as his assistant. George started out helping file and sort the photographs of the players, and soon he was out on the field taking pictures himself.

George's photographs have appeared in many magazines, newspapers, and baseball guides, as well as on baseball cards.

George Brace has taken pictures of 186 of the players now in the Baseball Hall of Fame in Cooperstown, New York. Through his photography, George has become part of the history of the game he loves so much.

Find Out More

Getting started

To be successful in sports communications you will need a college degree. You will also need to gain experience in your chosen field. There are classes and activities you can do now at your school or at a local community center. It's never too early to get started!

For future sportswriters:

Study the sports section in your local newspaper. Can you tell which pieces are columns? Which stories give opinions and sports analysis?

Watch a basketball or baseball game on television and write up the story. Then compare it with the story that appears in the morning paper.

Is there a school newspaper, newsletter, or yearbook you can help out on? Maybe you and your classmates can start one for your class.

For future sportscasters and announcers:

Does your school or community center offer drama classes? You will need to have a good speaking voice for this line of work.

Listen to the announcers while watching a game. Then try turning off the sound and tape-recording your own play by play.

For future public relations specialists:

Write to the public relations offices of your favorite professional teams and request a copy of their media guides. How are these books put together? What information do you think is helpful?

Volunteer to work on a school election or fund-raising campaign. What is the best way to get people to vote for your candidate or donate money to your school?

Start keeping a scrapbook on your favorite team. How can you use this to convince your friends that it is the best team?

For future photographers or camera operators:

Buy a good used manual camera and teach yourself the basics of focus, composition, and exposure, or sign up for photography or video-production classes at your school or a local art center. Ask if there is a darkroom you can learn to use.

Volunteer to take pictures at school sporting events for the school yearbook.

SPORTS

MEDICINE

W hen Bo Jackson was injured, everyone thought he would never play in sports again. But Bo was determined to get back on the playing field. Surgeons replaced his injured hip with an artificial one, and other sports medicine professionals worked with Bo to get him back into peak condition. Bo came back to play with the Chicago White Sox for the 1992–1993 season, and helped his team make it to the American League play-offs. There are thousands of sports medicine professionals who work day in and day out to keep athletes like Bo at the top of their sport.

What are the different jobs in sports medicine?

- Sports physicians keep athletes healthy, do physical checkups, and help players recover from injuries.

- Sports psychologists help athletes maintain a healthy state of mind.

- Athletic trainers plan conditioning programs for athletes and work with them to prevent injuries.

- Other professionals, like sports dentists, vision specialists, massage therapists, and nutritionists, all play important roles in helping athletes stay healthy and perform to the best of their abilities.

The job of a sports physician

Most M.D.s, or doctors of medicine, specialize in a particular field of medicine. One important specialization for an M.D. who wants to work with athletes is orthopedics. Orthopedic surgeons perform operations like the one Bo Jackson had. D.O.s, or doctors of osteopathic medicine, focus on the athlete's bones, muscles, ligaments, and nerves.

The job of a sports psychologist

The sports psychologist has two main goals: improving the performance and motivation of an athlete and helping the athlete with her or his personal problems. If an athlete is having a hard time making free throws, doing a gymnastic routine, or scoring the extra point, the psychologist will encourage the athlete to talk about what's bothering him or her. Psychologists also remind athletes that they are professionals with jobs to do.

The job of an athletic trainer

An athletic trainer is responsible for keeping the athletes healthy. The athletic trainer chooses the best equipment and workout routines for individuals and groups. The most important part of this job is injury prevention. The trainer helps athletes develop the strength and coordination to withstand the physical demands of competition. He or she is also involved in taping up the athletes if they need bandages or braces. If an athlete is injured, the trainer works with him or her to regain strength and fitness.

The job of a sports physical therapist

Physical therapists help athletes recover from injuries and improve their coordination and mobility. Physical therapists use electricity, heat, and ultrasound to relieve pain and improve muscle condition. An important part of their job is motivating athletes to do the exercises that will get them back in the game.

The training of a sports medicine professional

To become a sports physician, you must graduate from college, attend medical school for 4 years, and do follow-up work as a resident or intern at a hospital or clinic. The entire process can take 10 or more years. Sports psychologists must have a graduate degree in psychology. Physical therapists, trainers, nutritionists, and all the other professionals who work to keep athletes in good shape must take college courses in their specialty.

What is it like to work in sports medicine?

Sports physicians, psychologists, trainers, and others often travel to work with the athletes while they are on the road. A doctor might need to be on the field in case a player is injured, and will sometimes treat minor injuries right in the locker room. The massage therapist will be on hand to help relax athletes after particularly rough games. A psychologist will find a quiet place to talk with an athlete who is having problems on or off the field. Other doctors and psychologists who work with professional athletes have offices or work out of a hospital, keeping regular hours.

The pleasures and pressures of the job

The sports doctor, psychologist, or trainer might not be the one out on the basketball court, but that doesn't make a victory any less thrilling. After all, they've been directly involved in seeing to it that the athletes are in great physical and mental shape. Of course, you can't always be on the winning side. Because you work so closely with the athletes, injuries and setbacks present a challenge to you as well as to them.

Let's Meet...

Dr. Drayton R. Patterson
Sports Psychologist

Drayton Patterson is a former professional baseball player and scout, and is now a sports psychologist. His job keeps him close to the sport. He also works with children.

How did you get started?

Back when I was a ballplayer I used to practice some of the same techniques that I now teach athletes. I was always trying to find ways to enhance my own performance. After I injured my arm and couldn't pitch anymore, I worked as a scout with the Major League Scouting Bureau and the Texas Rangers. I would meet with young players and talk with them, and sometimes they would ask me for advice. When I got my Ph.D. I turned it into a profession.

Describe how you work with players.

The general manager of a baseball team might ask me to come and talk to one of the players who is having a hard time. I will go to meet with the athlete and encourage him to talk about what is bothering him. I will teach him how to remember previous experiences when he was successful. I will also teach him how to relax, because if you are tense you don't play well.

What training did you need?

I have a Ph.D. in psychology. I also like to think I have a Ph.D. in baseball. I've been an athlete, a scout, and now a psychologist. This background helps me gain the confidence of the players. I understand the highs and lows of the game, and what it feels like to compete. This is something that you can't learn from a book.

What do you like most about your job?

I enjoy helping athletes who are having a hard time concentrating, suffering from what I call "brain cramps," or making the same mistakes over and over. I like it when I can do something to help them let go of their tension. It's good knowing that I've helped them get their hits or make free throws or kick a field goal.

What is the hardest part of your job?

I am sometimes paid by the team and sometimes paid by the athlete. This depends on whoever made the initial contact with me. But I am also working privately with the player, and need to keep his problems and secrets confidential. The hardest part of my job is when I find out that a player has problems with drugs or alcohol. I need to decide whether I should keep this secret and help the player to help himself, or whether I should let management know what is going on. This decision, however, is made with the help of the athlete.

How Being a Former Baseball Player Helps Drayton Help Others

I think I can help players because I not only have expertise as a psychologist, but I also have learned from my own experiences as an athlete. Players trust me, and know that I understand what they are facing.

When I was scouting for the Texas Rangers I met with a kid who had good "stuff" but lacked confidence. He could pitch 86 to 90 miles per hour, but he could not throw a strike.

I told him that before games I wouldn't allow myself to think any negative thoughts. I would create an image in my head of where I wanted the ball to go. I had an image of my body doing what it needed to do to throw a curveball, a fastball, or whatever. I would imagine throwing perfect pitches or someone hitting into a double play.

I would prepare myself before I stepped onto the field, and that is how I programmed my body to perform. I worked with this kid and taught him how to use these techniques. He started throwing strikes, and later signed a professional contract.

Let's Meet...

Russ Riederer
Physical Development Coordinator

Russ Riederer is the physical development coordinator for the Chicago Bears. He is a certified strength and conditioning specialist.

What is your job?

My job is to make sure our football players are as physically developed as they can possibly be in their strength, flexibility, speed, power, agility, and cardiovascular endurance. I am the only one who works with the Bears, and I work with 60 players.

What preparation did you have for this job?

I went to college at Kansas State University, where I was a linebacker for 4 years on the college team. I studied physical education and exercise physiology. After I graduated, I coached at Kansas State for 8 years. After that I was the strength coach at Purdue for 4 years. I spent a year with the Green Bay Packers, and then I came to the Bears in January 1992.

What is your schedule like?

Over the year it changes. In-season starts in July at our training camp, and we play through January, if we go all the way. When we are in-season I get to work at 6:30 in the morning. I'll work with different players or groups all day until I go home at 6 in the evening. I try to make the workouts as individualized as I can, but sometimes I am working with 5 or 6 players or even 30 at a time. I also do the warm-up before every game, and during the game I do some recording of the defensive calls.

What kind of training do you do with the players?

During the season the players are working with strength training and power training. They warm up for 4 or 5 minutes, then go and do the different lifts that I have prescribed for them. I help them develop the areas of the body that will be most advantageous in being successful in the game of football. There is a 10-minute stretching routine that we go through with the entire team before we start practice every day.

What do you like most about your job?

The most enjoyment I get is when I see a guy develop and make himself better through the training. He gets faster, stronger, more flexible, and in overall better shape. Of course, this is a team sport made up of individuals, and the biggest satisfaction you can ever have is when they take that to the field as better players and it turns into wins.

How to Warm Up a Football Team

These are some of the warm-up routines that high school players should do before going on the field.

- Jog. This is a good way to loosen up the muscles and get your heart beating.
- Sprint. Begin with six to eight 5-yard sprints from a football stance. Then do the same with 10-yard sprints, working on increasing your stride. Finish up with four 20-yard sprints, concentrating on your running form.
- Run sideways. Run for 20 yards to your left, crossing your right leg over the left and then swinging your left leg wide to your left. Repeat to your right. Do this three times.
- Run backward. Do this three times, covering 20 yards each time.

Other exercises:

- While standing, raise one leg up, hold on to your shin, and slowly pull your knee and leg against your chest. Repeat with each leg six to eight times.
- Lie on your back and do the same stretch.
- Standing up, cross your feet and bend over from the waist and touch the ground while keeping your knees straight. Use an easy motion, taking care not to over-extend your knees. Repeat six to eight times, changing your feet.

Success Story

Dr. Dick Steadman

If you've ever skied, you know that alpine skiing can be a high-risk, high-speed sport. You've probably seen the terrifying tumbles of ski racers as they hurtle down the slopes during the Winter Olympics. When you see the snow fly as the skier goes head over heels, it comes as no surprise that these athletes often suffer broken bones.

J. Richard Steadman has been the chief physician of the U.S. Ski Team since 1976. He is one of the top orthopedic surgeons in the country, and is famous for his knee surgery and his skill at repairing even the most horribly fractured bones. He was also a pioneer in prescribing immediate, controlled exercises as soon as possible after surgery. Dick Steadman learned the value of exercise as a boy, and in high school he competed in football, basketball, and golf. He went on to play football at Texas A&M with coach Bear Bryant. When faced with a decision between football and medicine, Steadman chose to become a doctor. The members of the U.S. Ski Team are glad he did.

Find Out More

You and sports medicine

Are you fascinated by how the human body and mind operate? If you think dissecting a frog is gross, you might be too squeamish to consider a job as a sports doctor. But if you love science and respond well in emergency situations, you might enjoy medical school. The first 2 years are spent taking classes like anatomy, biochemistry, physiology, microbiology and pathology (the study of diseases). To become a doctor you need to be self-motivated and able to put up with extremely long and hard hours. After medical school, doctors must serve a residency, sometimes working 24 hours in a row, 80 hours a week.

Are you a good listener? A sports psychologist must be able to listen with an understanding and open mind. People pursuing a career in psychology must be emotionally stable, mature, and able to deal well with other people. You must also be patient and willing to stick with difficult situations. You must be a sensitive and compassionate person, and one who is able to lead and inspire others. You need strong verbal and writing skills to communicate with your clients and organizations.

Are you committed to keeping your own body in good shape? If so, you will be better able to help other people attain their physical goals, and might make a good trainer. Being a trainer requires patience, persuasiveness, and physical strength.

Do you like the idea of helping others? Be honest with yourself. Sports medicine requires an enormous amount of education and training, and you need to truly enjoy working closely with other people.

SPORTS

BUSINESS

Everywhere you turn you find evidence of our obsession with sports and recreation. Turn on the television and there's a game; open a magazine and there's an ad for sneakers. Walk down the street and you'll see a sports store or fitness club. While sports and recreation are definitely for fun, there's also an engine of business running beneath all the hoopla. The song says "Money makes the world go around," but it takes business managers and administrators to keep the gears in motion.

Jobs in sport and fitness management

In this chapter we'll meet a sports agent who represents professional basketball players, and the manager of a health club. While their jobs are very different, they both focus on the business side of sports. If you have an interest in business and a love of sports, some of the following jobs might interest you.

Sports marketing

Sports marketers are responsible for promoting sporting events through press releases, celebrity appearances, and media tours. They set up special sporting events to draw attention to the sport or team they are promoting; they arrange to place advertisements in magazines and on television and billboards. Professional teams hire sports marketers to help spread their name and fame beyond their home city.

Sports agents

If an athlete is talented enough to go professional, one of the most important actions he or she needs to take is selecting a sports agent. The agent will be responsible for managing the business side of the athlete's sports career. Agents negotiate players' contracts, give investment and tax advice, and help find advertising opportunities for their clients. The agent works for the athlete, and is usually paid a flat percentage (from 3 to 10 percent) of the athlete's salary and bonus. Agents who are attorneys usually charge a fee based on the number of hours spent negotiating and handling other aspects of the athlete's business.

Sports club management

Some of the oldest sports clubs are the large member-owned country clubs, yacht clubs, and tennis clubs. Most of the newer clubs are smaller athletic and fitness clubs, and more and more hotels and apartment buildings are adding sports facilities. There are also clubs like YWCAs and community swimming and tennis clubs. The manager of a sports club must find new members and oversee the operations of the facility.

Athletic directors

Most colleges and universities have athletic programs for their students. The athletic director is in charge of that program. He or she works with the faculty and staff of the university to provide athletic education and recreation for the college community. Running an athletic program is a lot like running a large business. The athletic director oversees the management of the sports facilities, hires the teachers and trainers, and organizes the exciting competitions that take place between colleges. An important part of this job is raising the money to support the athletic program.

Sports entrepreneurs

An entrepreneur is someone who organizes and manages a business undertaking, assuming the risk for the sake of the profit. These are the people who come up with an idea for a sports product and then find a way to get it into stores and, eventually, locker rooms, playing fields, and your home. The thing being sold might be a new kind of sneaker or an automatic pitching machine. Maybe it's a T-shirt, book, or sports video. Entrepreneurship requires innovation and creativity. A good entrepreneur is someone who knows what the public wants or needs.

Baseball scouts

For years, it was up to the baseball scout to find new talent and bring it to the attention of the professional sports teams. But the business of scouting has gone through many changes. Many young athletes make names for themselves while playing in high school and college, and the draft system determines which teams the best players go to.

But scouts still need to be able to
recognize and evaluate the talent of
young players in order to advise the
team management. The scouts also
find and sign amateur players for
the team's minor league systems.
Many baseball scouts start out as
baseball players themselves, a
background that helps them iden-
tify good players.

Let's Meet...

Henry Thomas
Sports Agent

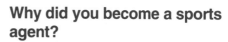

Henry Thomas is an agent for professional basketball players. His main responsibility as an agent is to negotiate the player's contract with his team.

Why did you become a sports agent?

I grew up in sports, so I knew that after I became a lawyer I would try to tie what I was doing profession-ally to what I truly love. I started teaching a sports law class at a law school about 10 years ago. I wanted to be prepared when the opportu-nity came along to represent a professional athlete.

How do you get to be an agent?

You really become an agent by getting the clients. The professional team sports have unions that repre-sent all the players; to negotiate a player contract, you need to be certified, by providing the union with background information on yourself.

How do you get clients?

The best way is to be around the sport. Or if you grew up in the same neighborhood as the player, or know

someone in that neighborhood, chances are you'll at least have the opportunity to meet the player. You can establish a relationship, and perhaps one day convince the player that you should be his or her representative.

What does it take to be a good agent?

You need to have integrity and be responsible and conscientious about what you do. The specific things you need to know, like the market value of particular players, you can pick up. It helps to have negotiating skills and good communication skills as well.

What are some of the pressures?

You need to be constantly recruiting so you can add to your client list. You also need to work hard to maintain the relationships that you already have. It's a cutthroat business.

What is your life as an agent like?

I travel a lot, scouting for players that I think have potential. I need to stay visible. I'm often on the phone well into the night, because I'm dealing with people who are younger than me, and who tend to be up late. Plus I've found that if you are trying to get new clients, it's best to communicate with them outside of normal business hours.

What do you like the most about being an agent?

It's gratifying to watch a young man develop and mature into a responsible adult.

Giving Back to the Community

For Henry Thomas, being an agent means not only negotiating an athlete's contract, but being involved in other aspects of the player's public life. This can often be very rewarding.

"I'm Tim Hardaway's agent. Sometimes athletes enjoy success but forget where they came from and don't go back and try to help some of the younger people along. But Tim has a scholarship in his name at Carver High School that goes to the top student athlete every year, to pay for college. That comes out of his own money.

"Tim's high school coach died of cancer a couple of years after Tim got to college. Now that Tim plays in the NBA, every time Tim gets an assist in a game he donates money to the American Cancer Society. We went out and got corporations in the San Francisco Bay area to match his contributions with donations of their own.

"I think all professional athletes should do something like this. They are very fortunate that their profession pays a lot of money. Very few young men are good enough or lucky enough to play at that level and make that kind of money. I think there is a responsibility to give back to their communities."

Let's Meet...

Walter Gray
Health Club Manager

Walter Gray is the weekend manager at an athletic club. He is responsible for hiring the people who work at the club. He also finds new members and helps them with their workout routines.

How did you get the job?

I started working in the club as a sales manager. My job was to bring business to the club. Once I got here I fit in perfectly, and soon my employers found out I was capable of doing other jobs. They started giving me added responsibilities. After about 3 months I got into doing personal training, and then I was promoted to weekend manager.

Why do you think you are suited to this job?

I've always been very into sports. I played football and basketball in high school, and I also ran track. I studied physical education for 2 years in college, and later on I played Baker League basketball in Philadelphia with a few of the old NBA stars. I also enjoy business, and I'd like to be in my own sports-related business one day.

Did you have any special training?

I learned a lot about athletics when I was participating in sports myself. But I had to do a lot of on-the-job training. I needed to read up on the various pieces of machinery and learn about the muscles of the human body. I needed to know which machines would work which muscles, so I could teach our members.

What do you like the most about your job?

I like being in a totally athletic environment. I can work out as much as I want. I also have the opportunity to work with kids who like sports but who might not have a lot of guidance. I can provide some of that guidance, and athletics helps keep them off the street.

What are some of the pressures?

The pressure in this job comes from the sales part. I need to interview new members, give them tours of the club, and sign them up, as well as working with the employees, training, and making sure the club is run right. I knew that pressure would come with the job, but that's when I'm at my best, when my back's against the wall.

What does it take to be a good health club manager?

You need to set a good example, so that people will respect and follow you. You need to be athletically oriented. When things happen that people don't understand, they come to you for answers. If you don't have the answers, you need to have the resources to get them.

A Typical Day for Walter Gray

I come in in the morning and check my mailbox for messages. People call me with problems about their membership or about their work-out. They might want to see the trainer for a new workout. I'll work on the books to schedule their appointments.

Then I go through the club to make sure that the regular maintenance routines have been done. I check for cleanliness and to make sure everything is in order. I go downstairs to the free-weight areas and work with the people there. If I see somebody who isn't using the weights right, I'll show him or her how to do the exercises properly.

Then I come back to my office, return phone calls, and schedule the rest of the appointments. I set up touring times for people who are interested in checking out the club. For the rest of my shift I just do what needs to be done. I need to be able to solve the problems that come up on an average day, train the staff, and make sure the club is a nice place for people to exercise.

Success Stories

Mark Hume McCormack

Mark McCormack started playing golf as therapy after he fractured his skull in an auto acci-
dent. He was good enough to win
the Chicago prep title and went
on to play for the College of William and Mary. He studied
at Yale Law School, but maintained his love of golf. While
working as a lawyer, Mark McCormack began developing
his business as a sports entrepreneur, arranging exhibitions
for professional golfers. When he struck out on his own as a
sports agent in 1960, he started with one client, Arnold
Palmer, and the conviction that businesses and corporations
would be glad to pay to have their names associated with
star athletes. In the years since then Mark McCormack has
built a powerful sports management company, with offices
in 20 countries. More than 1,000 people work for his Inter-
national Management Group. Star clients include Andre
Agassi, Martina Navratilova, and Greg Norman. Mark
McCormack is known for his imagination, competitiveness,
and attention to detail. He has written several books, including the best-selling *What They Don't Teach You at
Harvard Business School.*

Sonny Vaccaro didn't take the straight road to success, but he nevertheless got where he wanted to be. Growing up in Trafford, Pennsylvania, Sonny sold vegetables and fruit and was a high school football star and baseball player. He turned down an offer to play with the Pittsburgh Pirates because he had promised his father he'd go to college. After graduating, Sonny Vaccaro worked as a teacher and coach, organized the first national high school all-star basketball game, and even tried his hand as a sports agent. His true love had always been basketball, and in the late 1970s he came up with some ideas for a better basketball shoe. He took his samples to Nike, and although his shoe designs flopped he was given a job in the promotions department, where he made his mark on the world of sports business. His strategy? Convincing high school and college coaches to put their players in Nike sneakers, provided free by the company. In return, Nike got added visibility and publicity. Sonny Vaccaro was also involved in getting Michael Jordan to come aboard the Nike team. Sonny Vaccaro has been instrumental in making the Nike "swoosh" logo a symbol recognized around the world.

Find Out More

You and a career in sports business

- Interview a manager at a local sports club. How many hours a week does he or she work? What does the job involve? Is there anything you can do to help out?

- Meet with an athletic official who is in charge of a special event (a local tennis tournament or a bicycle race) and volunteer to help. Keep a record of the various tasks involved in putting together a sporting event.

- Interview people who have developed or are selling a sports product. How did they get started? Where did they get the money to develop their product? What has made them successful? What would they avoid next time?

- Prepare a sales strategy for an imaginary sports product. Better yet, see if you can come up with an idea for a new product. Your first few ideas might not pan out, but keep trying.

- Read, read, read. Study *Sports Illustrated* and other sources of sports news information. If you want to be an agent, become a student of the game you want to work in.

BALLPARKS
&
STADIUMS

H ot dogs! Peanuts! There's more to a ball game than home runs and line drives. Next time you go to a stadium or ballpark, look around to see how many people are working there. At a big park, there will be more than 500 people who work together to put on the show. You'll see people at the ticket windows and vendors selling food and souvenirs. You'll hear an announcer calling the plays and an organ player setting the mood. Day in and day out there are people who are working in ballparks and stadiums, preparing for the arrival of the players and fans. In this chapter you'll find out about some of the jobs behind the scenes.

What it's like to work at a sports facility

Working at a sports facility is definitely not the job for a hermit! Many of the jobs you find in stadiums and ballparks have something in common with jobs you find all over. There are people serving food, sweeping floors, working on computers, maintaining public order, and keeping the grass green. But there's a big difference between working in a stadium and working in an office building: the crowds. The people who work in a sports facility must know their specific tasks and be able to concentrate despite the noise and pressure.

Maintaining the playing field

Groundskeepers at athletic fields must keep the natural or artificial turf in perfect condition for competitions. For example, on the day of a baseball game, the grounds crew rolls up the cover that protects the infield from rain and rolls the dirt flat. The grass in the outfield is watered and mowed, and the white foul lines are put down with a paint machine. Then the pitcher's mound is raked smooth, and water is sprinkled on the infield. After the fifth inning, the grounds crew smooths over the base paths again.

The ticket office

At Boston's Fenway Park, the tickct office employs 35 people who sell tickets over the phone or directly to the fans who come to the ticket office. And Fenway Park is the smallest of the big-league baseball stadiums, with only 33,925 seats! The people who work in the ticket office must also enter all ticket information into computers and add up the money. When the gates open at Fenway, ticket-takers take their places at the entry gates. On game days each person might rip 2,300 tickets, while quickly checking to make sure each one is valid.

Equipment managers

The equipment manager for a baseball team is responsible for making sure that the players have clean uniforms and equipment and that the clubhouse is stocked with food and newspapers. When the team is going on the road, it is up to the equipment manager to pack all the necessary gear. On a basketball team, the equipment manager organizes the luggage, ice bags, prewraps, uniforms, and towels. He or she also gets one of the best seats in the house, right behind the bench. During a game the equip-ment manager must be on hand to provide the players with ice packs, fresh towels, and refreshments.

Concession stands

Selling food and souvenirs to the public is an important source of money in the sports business. Concession operators have contracts with the owners of the stadium and give them a portion of the money they make. Some of the food is sold from stands, while other food vendors walk up and down the aisles. Other vendors walk through the park selling souvenirs and programs. At the end of the day they turn in their unsold merchandise and the money they have collected. How much these roving vendors get paid will depend on how much they have sold. So it's no wonder that they shout so loudly!

Mascots and cheerleaders

More than half of the NBA teams have mascots, like the Gorilla from Phoenix or Harry the Hawk from Atlanta. At halftime and time-outs, mascots and cheerleaders entertain the crowds with their acrobatics or clownish routines. Off court, mascots attend fund-raisers and make visits to children's hospitals and other charitable organizations. The people who fill these costumes are often athletes in their own right, with training in gymnastics and acrobatics.

Some other jobs at stadiums and ballparks

- Scoreboard operators
- Maintenance crews
- Public announcers
- Organ players and band members
- Referees and umpires
- Security guards
- Computer technicians

Things you can do to get a head start

There are many places where you can volunteer to work close to sports. The best place to start is with the varsity teams at your own school, or at the tennis matches and other sporting events at your community center. If you would like to make a little extra money, talk to the people who run concession stands at the stadium near you.

Let's Meet...

Nancy Faust
Organ Player

Nancy Faust has been the official organist for the Chicago White Sox since 1970; she plays at every game in Comiskey Park. She has also played the organ for the Bulls, the Sting, and the Blackhawks.

How did you get started?

I've played the organ since I was 4 years old, and I could always pick out tunes by ear. After college, my friends who were sports enthusiasts encouraged me to write to all the sports teams in Chicago and ask for a job. A year later the White Sox office called and offered me the job.

What do you do on game days?

I get to the park 1½ or 2 hours before the game and eat at the press dinner the White Sox put on for people from the newspapers, television, and radio. I start playing an hour before the game, while the fans are coming in. I wear a headset and listen to the scoreboard director, who tells me what will be put on the board and when to stop for announcements. Once the game starts I play songs that reflect the situation on the field. When someone is walked I might play "Ease on Down the Road" or "Follow the

Yellow Brick Road." I play different songs for different players, and I also play the "trickle-down" sound—it ends in a "pop"—when the ball is fouled back onto the nets.

What do you like most about your job?

I like that people are out at the park enjoying themselves, and I like being part of that. It's fun to get the fans going with "Zorba the Greek" and "Charge." I also like the contact with people. When the Sox built the new stadium I was told I could be in a booth away from the crowd, but I like where I am, near the box seats. I turn around and people are looking in and talking to me. I like being accessible.

What do you like least about your job?

I feel a lot of pressure to come up with good ideas. I am always listening for new songs to play, and then I need to learn them. That can be stressful, because I like to get a song for all the players from the visiting teams. I also hate long rain delays when we come back to lose. And my job isn't easy to get to. There's always lots of traffic.

What should kids do who want to do what you do?

There aren't many jobs doing exactly what I do. To do this you need to have a really good ear and to be constantly expanding your repertoire. Listen to games and pretend you are playing, and see what songs you can come up with.

Where Does Nancy Get Her Ideas?

Nancy is always listening to new music, trying to come up with the perfect jingle for the White Sox and for visiting players. So when Bo Jackson started playing again after his hip surgery, she played "Feelin' Stronger Every Day" and "Hip to Be Square" when he walked on the field. She played "Love Potion Number Nine" for John Olerud, because he wears 9 for the Toronto Blue Jays. Sometimes she gets her ideas from television. For the Seattle Mariners' Ken Griffey, Jr. she played the theme from "The Andy Griffith Show." Other songs from TV shows:

- The "Flipper" song for a player named Salmon.

- "The Brady Bunch" for a batter whose first name was Greg, since one of the boys on the show is named Greg.

- The "Star Trek" theme for Kirk McCaskill, in honor of Captain Kirk of the Starship Enterprise.

- "Three's Company" for a player wearing the number 3.

   People in the audience often give Nancy great ideas, like the one for Captain Kirk. Next time you go to a ballpark and you have an idea for a song to go with a ballplayer, go tell it to the organist.

Let's Meet...

Daniel Ahearn
Operations Manager

Daniel Ahearn is in charge of operations at a large city indoor stadium.

What does your job involve?

I'm responsible for installing and maintaining the ice and maintaining and operating the resurfacing machine. I supervise the work crew for the changeovers, when we go from an ice rink to a basketball court, and when we need to set up for ice shows, the circus, or a concert.

What steps are involved in installing the ice?

First we turn the refrigeration plant on. It's in the basement, and it runs a coolant through pipes that are under the floor. We spray a thin coat of water on the floor with a hose, and then we go into the painting process. A coat of titanium dioxide paint gives the ice the white color. We seal that with a clear coat of water, and then we paint the lines, circles, and logos onto the ice. We seal that layer and start flooding the rink with a fire hose until

the ice gets to be about half an inch thick.
That's when we bring in the Zamboni with the
hot water to put another half inch on.

What does the Zamboni do?

The Zamboni is a resurfacing machine. It has
an adjustable knife that shaves the ice. It also
has a conveyor system that collects the shav-
ings and the snow from skating. Behind the
cutting knife there's the wash-water system.
Cold water comes out and washes the ice, and
a pickup pump recycles that; then out the back
of the machine comes hot water to put a fresh
water surface on the ice.

How did you learn to do your job?

I started working in an ice rink when I was
10 years old because I needed money to play
hockey and to buy hockey equipment. I started
out as an ice rink guard. One day when I was
14 years old the guy who was supposed to
work the resurfacer didn't show up, so I drove
it out on the ice for the first time. After that
I would run the machine on the ice when the
supervisor was there.

What do you like about your job?

I like being able to watch all the hockey
games, and getting to know the players. Also
I'm very mechanical and I like working on the
equipment. Also, sometimes I get to skate at
the stadium. I played hockey all my life, but
I had to quit after I demolished my knee. But
I still like to get out on the ice.

A Day on the Job with Daniel Ahearn

- Get to work at 8:30 A.M.; get the machine ready to resurface the ice before practice.

- Resurface for 10:30 practice; get the machine ready again, refilling it with water.

- Resurface for visiting team's practice at 11:30; then get the ice ready for the game.

- Run the edger along the side of the rink. (The Zamboni doesn't get all the way out to the sides.)

- Crew goes out and knocks the ice chips off the dasher boards where the edger was.

- Flood the ice.

By then it's 2 o'clock, and Dan can take a break for an hour or so. By 4, he starts getting ready for the game.

- Drill the holes in the ice for the net moorings.

- Fill the machine up again and resurface the ice at 5.

- Work crew reports at 6 P.M. Give them instructions for the evening (sweeping, setting up the nets).

- Players take the ice at 6:50 for a 20-minute pregame skate.

- Resurface the ice for game.

- Game starts at 7:30.

- Resurface before the second and third periods.

Success Stories

Sherry Davis

Sherry Davis is a serious baseball fan. Some years she has gone to more than 60 games a season. But Sherry doesn't need to buy a ticket anymore. In 1993 she became the first full-time female public address announcer in major league baseball. Sherry had a drama degree from the College of Notre Dame of Maryland in Baltimore; after graduating she worked for a while in regional theatre and commercial voice-overs and as an extra in a few movies. She was working as a legal secretary in San Francisco when she heard about the auditions at Candlestick Park, and decided to try out. These days her warm and friendly voice sets the mood for San Francisco Giants games.

Ted Spencer

You might say that Ted Spencer was born to work in baseball: His parents named him after Ted Williams, one of the greatest to ever play the game. Ted Spencer studied industrial design in college and went on to work in graphic design and video production. But when he saw an ad for the job as curator at the Baseball Hall of Fame in Cooperstown, New York, he knew he had found the perfect situation. As curator, Ted designs and installs the exhibits that illustrate the past and present of baseball.

Find Out More

You and jobs in sports facilities

Does spending your free time at a baseball field or stadium sound right for you? As Daniel Ahearn's story shows, there are plenty of opportunities for young people who are willing to work hard. Your first step toward a job with a professional team or in a large sports facility might be working in a small ice rink or at a local gym.

Another good place to look for experience is with a minor league baseball team. All the major league teams have a system of farm teams in the minor leagues, and for each minor league team there is a stadium. Baseball players usually begin their careers in the rookie leagues, moving up to play in the Class A league, then Class AA, and finally Class AAA, which is just below the majors. Most professional teams also operate spring training camps. (If there is a football training camp near your home, ask about opportunities there, too.)

Rookie leagues include:

Appalachian League (teams in West Virginia, North Carolina, and Tennessee)
157 Carson Lane
Bristol, VA 24201

Pioneer League (teams in Montana,
    Idaho, Utah, and Alberta,
    Canada)
P.O. Box 1144
Billings, MT 59301

Class A leagues include:

The Northwest Baseball League
P.O. Box 30025
Portland, OR 97230

The Midwest Baseball League
P.O. Box 936
Beloit, WI 53511

The South Atlantic Baseball League
504 Crescent Hill
P.O. Box 38
King's Mountain, NC 28086

The California Baseball League
1060 Willow St.
P.O. Box 26400
San Jose, CA 95215

INDEX